LET'S GO HUNTING

Hunting DUCKS

Hines Lambert

PowerKiDS press
New York

Published in 2013 by The Rosen Publishing Group, Inc.
29 East 21st Street, New York, NY 10010

First Edition

Editor: Amelie von Zumbusch
Book Design: Kate Laczynski

Photo Credits: Background graphic © iStockphoto.com/Andrea Zanchi; sidebar binoculars © iStockphoto.com/Feng Yu; cover Regina Usher/age fotostock/Getty Images; pp. 5, 15 Kansas City Star/McClatchy-Tribune/Getty Images; p. 6 ebrom/Shutterstock.com; p. 7 Jean Orrico/Shutterstock.com; p. 8 (left) Mark Anderson/USFWS; p. 8 (right) Richard C. Clifton/USFWS; p. 9 Robbie George/National Geographic/Getty Images; pp. 10, 27 iStockphoto/Thinkstock; p. 11 Miami Herald/McClatchy-Tribune/Getty Images; pp. 12, 17 Jens Stolt/Shutterstock.com; p. 13 auremar/Shutterstock.com; p. 14 Teresa Levite/Shutterstock.com; p. 16 Nick Ridley/Oxford Scientific/Getty Images; p. 18 Konjushenko Vladimir/Shutterstock.com; p. 19 Hemera/Thinkstcock; p. 20 (left) Glenn Price/Shutterstock.com; p. 20 (right) S. Solum/PhotoLink/Photodisc/Getty Images; p. 21 Edwin Remsberg/Taxi/Getty Images; p. 23 Suzi Nelson/Shutterstock.com; p. 24 Tacoma News Tribune/McClatchy-Tribune/Getty Images; p. 25 Kelly Nelson/Shutterstock.com; p. 26 Kirk Geisler/Shutterstock.com; p. 28 Ryan Hagerty/USFWS.

Library of Congress Cataloging-in-Publication Data

Lambert, Hines.
Hunting ducks / by Hines Lambert. — 1st ed.
p. cm. — (Let's go hunting)
Includes index.
ISBN 978-1-4488-9661-5 (library binding) — ISBN 978-1-4488-9780-3 (pbk.) —
ISBN 978-1-4488-9781-0 (6-pack)
1. Duck shooting—Juvenile literature. I. Title.
SK333.D8L36 2013
799.2'44—dc23

2012025702

Manufactured in the United States of America

CPSIA Compliance Information: Batch #W13PK2: For Further Information contact Rosen Publishing, New York, New York at 1-800-237-9932

CONTENTS

Saving the Ducks

Duck hunting is one of the most popular sports in the world. It is no wonder because ducks can live in so many **habitats**. They are one of the few animals that can be found on every continent except Antarctica.

Hunting has a long history in the United States. Both Native Americans and settlers from other lands hunted ducks. Not only was duck hunting fun, it was also a great way to feed their families. In fact, duck hunting was so popular that the birds nearly died out. Congress voted to save the duck in 1918 by passing the **Migratory** Bird Treaty Act. This act created laws like hunting seasons and **bag limits**. Thanks to these laws, we can still enjoy hunting ducks today.

Duck hunters enjoy being outdoors, practicing their skills, and learning about these beautiful birds.

Dabblers and Divers

Ducks can be found almost everywhere. There are 28 **species** of ducks in North America. Most of these ducks are divided into two main types called dabblers, or dabbling ducks, and divers, or diving ducks. Dabblers live near beaches or shallow waters. Divers get their name because they can dive into deep water for food.

Ducks migrate with the seasons. Good hunters know when and where ducks migrate. Your state's

Mallard ducks are the most common kind of duck throughout the Northern Hemisphere, or half of Earth.

Many ducks, such as the wood duck here, have beautiful plumage, or feathers. Males tend to be more colorful than females.

wildlife office can help you figure out when they pass through your area. It will also tell you about your state's duck hunting laws. Some rules are so important that they are laws in almost every state. For example, good hunters never shoot "sitting ducks," or ducks that are swimming. Most hunters believe that shooting at a sitting duck is cheating.

Did You Know?

A duck's feet have no nerves or blood vessels. This means that a duck can swim in freezing water without its feet getting cold.

Duck Stamps

The US government puts out new duck stamps each year.

Even though hunters try to kill a few ducks, many of them respect nature and admire the beauty of the birds that they hunt. Some hunters work hard to protect ducks and their habitats. One simple way to protect ducks is by purchasing duck stamps. Duck stamps are exactly what they sound like. They are stamps that show pictures of ducks. You cannot use them to send

a letter, but every duck stamp you buy raises money to help save **wetlands** and other places ducks spend time.

Duck stamps were first used as hunting **licenses**, but they got too popular. People wanted to buy hundreds of them just to own them. Over the years, duck stamps have raised more than $750 million to help ducks!

Did You Know?

Wetlands are not only important because they are ducks' habitat. Wetlands actually clean water before it goes into rivers or the ocean.

The money raised by selling duck stamps helps fund wildlife refuges across the United States. These canvasback ducks are in Mattamuskeet National Wildlife Refuge, in Swan Quarter, North Carolina.

Camouflage and Waders

Before you go hunting, it is important to pick the right clothing. Unlike many **game** animals, ducks have excellent vision. This means that wearing **camouflage** is a must. Brown camouflage patterns are better than green ones because ducks see the color green very well.

Waders keep you dry in the wetlands where ducks are most often found.

Ducks can spot even a tiny piece of your skin. Camouflage your whole body, including your face.

Waders are almost as important as camouflage. These are waterproof boots that usually go all the way up to your chest. They look like rubber overalls. Waders help hunters retrieve their kills. They also come in handy when getting in and out of a boat. Many hunters get special **insulated** waders to keep warm. Along with a camouflage outfit and waders, it is always wise to bring good **binoculars**.

Boats

Make sure that your boat is big enough to hold both you and your hunting gear.

While most animals are hunted on dry land, duck hunters often hunt from boats. Some hunters prefer simple, lightweight boats that are easy to carry and steer. Many even use canoes or kayaks, which are very light and easy to transport.

Jon boats have a special design that is great for duck hunting. Jon boats are flat with benches. They are made especially for calm water, such as lakes and ponds.

Another boating option is an airboat. Airboats can carry several people, lots of gear, and dogs. Some can go on both land and water.

Obey safety rules when hunting in boats. Young hunters should always wear life vests. More duck hunters die each year from water accidents than from gun accidents!

Did You Know?

Did you know that it is illegal to hunt from a moving boat? If you want to hunt, your boat must be motionless, with its engine off or its sail furled.

If you bring a hunting dog in a boat with you, you need to be extra careful.

Blinds

Remember, ducks have excellent vision. They will avoid hunters if they see them. The best duck hunters avoid being seen. This is when blinds come in handy. A blind is like a camouflage shield that helps the hunter hide from ducks.

Some hunters prefer to make their own blinds. They often use reeds and plants. Some dig holes to hide inside.

This duck-hunting blind is covered in reeds and grasses that grew in the nearby marsh.

These young hunters are using a permanent blind for their duck hunt in western Missouri.

Many hunters buy blinds at sporting stores. There are all kinds. Some are small screens. Others are large and look like tents or huts. These blinds work well in cold weather. There are even large blinds that can completely camouflage boats. It is a good idea to visit your hunting spot to see what kind of blind might work best for you.

Shotguns

Although some states allow duck hunting with bows, most hunters prefer using **shotguns**. Shooting a moving bird with an arrow is far too difficult! **Rifles** are not safe for duck hunting because they shoot too far. A shotgun is perfect for hunting ducks. When you fire a shotgun, it scatters little tiny pellets, or shot. Shot makes it easier to hit a moving target.

Experienced hunters can give you good advice about different kinds of shotguns. Double-barreled shotguns, such as this one, have two barrels.

The **gauge** is a measure of a shotgun's power. This is simply the width of the barrel. The most popular gauge for duck hunting is the .12 gauge. Most shotguns can hold several shells to allow hunters to shoot several ducks without reloading. This also comes in handy if you miss.

Try to use special shells that will not harm the ducks' habitat. One kind of safer shell uses steel shot instead of lead.

Did You Know?

You must be a quick shooter to hunt ducks! They can fly as fast as 60 miles per hour (97 km/h)! They travel far in one day, but then they must rest and eat for a few days.

Practice Makes Perfect

It's a good idea to practice shooting before you go hunting. One of the biggest mistakes that beginners tend to make is shooting at ducks when they are too far away. When this happens, the shot is too weak to kill the ducks quickly. This causes them to die slowly and painfully. Hunters often cannot even locate ducks that they shoot from a great distance. Good hunters wait until the duck is 25 to 30 yards (23–27 m) away. A duck is within range if you can see its eyes.

Do not shoot at a duck unless you think that you will be able to kill it cleanly.

When it is not hunting season, some duck hunters shoot trap to work on their aim. In this sport, people try to hit disks, called clay pigeons, which have been fired into the air.

Ducks often fly together in large groups. It is best to aim for the last bird in the line. If that bird falls, shoot the next one at the end of the line. Shooting clubs provide a safe place to practice.

Decoys

Decoys offer one clever way to outsmart ducks. Decoys are fakes, or statues, of ducks that were designed to attract other birds to them. Ducks feel safe around other ducks. A decoy can fool a duck into thinking a particular area has food. Sometimes male ducks are looking for mates. A decoy of a female duck can attract male ducks.

Good duck decoys look like ducks of a specific species. This decoy (below) and real duck (left) are buffleheads.

Making duck decoys takes a lot of time and talent.

The first duck decoys were made from wood. Today, plastic decoys are very popular. Each decoy is painted in great detail to look just like the right species of duck. Decoys can be quite lifelike and beautiful. Some people even collect old decoys. In 2007, a very old duck decoy sold for more than $1 million!

Seeing Is Believing

There is more to using decoys than just putting them in the water. The way they are arranged must look as real as possible in order to fool actual ducks. Many hunters set up decoys in a spread. Good spreads are based on how real ducks group themselves and behave around each other.

Moving decoys also look very real. Some hunters attach strings to their decoys so they can tug them. Others place the decoys in moving water. You might try mixing the species of decoys. For example, mallard ducks feel very safe around geese. Goose decoys might help you hunt mallards.

Even the best decoys cannot help hunters if no ducks are around. Picking a good hunting spot is the most important step.

This hunter is using a wood duck decoy (left) and several mallard decoys.

Hearing Is Believing

Hunters can also outsmart ducks by making special sounds called duck calls. Ducks make different noises at different times. It is important to study actual duck calls so that you know what real ducks sound like. Most ducks speak in four or five short quacks.

Tools called duck calls can help hunters make duck noises. Some duck calls look like whistles. They fit easily in pockets. When hunters see ducks in flight, they

The first whistle-like calls were likely made in the Midwest around 1850.

Good duck calls sound almost exactly like real ducks.

can bring them closer by using calls. The idea is to trick ducks into thinking you are a duck in a safe area with lots of food.

You must be patient when calling a flock of ducks. Sometimes a few birds will break off from the group and fly closer to the water. Don't put your call away until the entire flock has flown by.

Did You Know?

If you are making your own calls, tape yourself calling and then listen. Make sure you sound like a real duck.

Dogs

Good retrievers carry birds firmly but gently in their mouths.

Many hunters enjoy duck hunting with their dogs. Different breeds of dogs are good at hunting particular animals. Retrievers, such as Labrador and golden retrievers, are great at hunting ducks. These dogs are excellent swimmers. They even have webbed paws. They got their name because they love to retrieve.

Retrievers can be trained to fetch dead ducks just as they can be trained to fetch balls and sticks.

It is important to train dogs before they join a duck hunt. An untrained dog might retrieve decoys. It is also good to practice duck calls with dogs so they do not get confused when they hear calls on the hunt. Dogs are far better at finding and retrieving ducks than humans. It is important not to waste ducks by leaving dead ones behind.

This man is training his dog to retrieve ducks. If you want to hunt with a dog, it is important to train it properly.

A Duck's Best Friend

Over the years, hunters have proven themselves to be good friends to ducks. By the early 1900s, ducks and their habitats were in serious trouble. There were no bag limits, so hunters could shoot as many ducks as they liked. Businesses destroyed habitats to make room for new buildings.

Ducks Unlimited was created in 1937 to protect duck habitats. It is an organization made up of duck hunters. Some people believe that hunters do not care about the **environment**. Ducks Unlimited proves that they do. It has saved more than 4.5 million acres (1.8 million ha) and countless ducks. Thanks to Ducks Unlimited, duck hunting is still one of the most popular sports in America. If you enjoy duck hunting, you might think about joining Ducks Unlimited. You can learn more at www.ducks.org.

Duck hunters get to spend time in beautiful natural areas. These hunters are in Alaska's Izembek National Wildlife Refuge.

HUNTING TIPS

1. If a flock spots you, stay very still. Movement might scare the ducks away.

2. Ducks can see through bad camouflage patterns. Check with sporting stores to find the best camouflage.

3. Make sure your decoy isn't shiny. Ducks will be suspicious of a decoy that shines.

4. Get there early! If you set up before sunrise, you won't scare the ducks.

5. There is an old saying, "Only call to tips and tails." If a duck is coming straight toward you, you don't need to call it.

6. If it is cold, your duck call might freeze. Spray it with a weather-resistant polish.

7. If you are in shallow water, kick some mud up around your decoys. A muddy area is easy to see from a flying duck's point of view.

8. Ducks prefer smaller bodies of water at the end of the day. If you live near only small ponds, go hunting in the afternoon.

GLOSSARY

bag limits (BAG LIH-muts) How many of certain kinds of animals hunters are allowed to kill.

binoculars (bih-NAH-kyuh-lurz) Handheld lenses that make things seem closer.

camouflage (KA-muh-flahj) A color or a pattern that matches the surroundings and helps hide something.

environment (en-VY-ern-ment) Everything that surrounds people and other living things and everything that makes it possible for them to live.

game (GAYM) Wild animals that are hunted for food.

gauge (GAYJ) The measure of how wide the barrel of a gun is.

habitats (HA-buh-tats) The kinds of land where animals or plants naturally live.

insulated (IN-suh-lay-ted) Covered with something that stops heat or sound from flowing out.

licenses (LY-sun-sez) Official permissions to do something.

migratory (MY-gruh-tor-ee) Moving from one place to another.

rifles (RY-fulz) Long guns that are fired from the shoulder.

shotguns (SHOT-gunz) Guns with smooth insides that are fired from the shoulder.

species (SPEE-sheez) One kind of living thing. All people are one species.

wetlands (WET-landz) Land with a lot of wetness in the soil.

INDEX

WEBSITES

Due to the changing nature of Internet links, PowerKids Press has developed an online list of websites related to the subject of this book. This site is updated regularly. Please use this link to access the list:
www.powerkidslinks.com/lgh/duck/